The Search for Poison-Dart Frogs

Ron Fridell

A Wildlife Conservation Society Book

Franklin Watts
A Division of Scholastic Inc.
New York • Toronto • London • Auckland • Sydney
Mexico City • New Delhi • Hong Kong
Danbury, Connecticut

The Wildlife Conservation Society (WCS) is dedicated to protecting and promoting the world's wildlife and wilderness areas. Founded in 1895 as the New York Zoological Society, the organization operates the Bronx Zoo, New York Aquarium, Central Park Wildlife Center, Queens Wildlife Center, and Prospect Park Wildlife Center. WCS also operates St. Catherines Wildlife Center, which is located off the coast of Georgia. The scientists at this center raise and study a variety of threatened and endangered animals.

WCS currently sponsors more than 350 field projects in 52 countries. The goal of these projects is to save wild landscapes and the animals that depend on them. In addition, WCS's pioneering environmental education programs reach more than 3 million students in the New York metropolitan area and are used in all 50 states and 14 foreign nations.

Library of Congress Cataloging-in-Publication Data

Fridell, Ron.
    The search for poison-dart frogs / Ron Fridell.
        p. cm.—(A Wildlife Conservation Society Book)
    Includes bibliographical references and index.
    ISBN 0-531-11888-6 (lib. bdg.)   0-531-16570-1 (pbk.)
    1. Dendrobatidae—Suriname—Juvenile literature. 2. Wildlife conservation—Suriname—Juvenile literature. [1. Wildlife conservation. 2. Poison frogs. 3. Frogs. 4. Zoologists. 5. Suriname—Description and travel.] I. Title.

QL668.E233 F75   2001
597.8'77'09883—dc21   00-036507

Contents

Meet the Author

Ron Fridell poses for a photo near his home in Evanston, Illinois.

Ron Fridell lives in Evanston, Illinois, with his wife Patricia, and their dog, an Australian shepherd named Madeline. He has written for radio, TV, newspapers, and textbooks. He has also taught English as a second language in Bangkok, Thailand, as a member of the peace corps.

According to Ron, "The idea for this book started with my friend, Nan Simpson. Nan raises frogs. She keeps them in terrariums in her living room in Evanston, Illinois. Nan knows I like frogs too. When I was writing my first book about frogs, *Amphibians in Danger: A Worldwide Warning*, she showed me a magazine article about a wildlife biologist searching for poison-dart frogs in Ecuador. That biologist was Ron Gagliardo.

"Ron Gagliardo's article made me curious about poison-dart frogs. I wanted to find out more about them. His e-mail address was included in the article, so I wrote to him.

"He replied and told me about other trips he'd taken to look for and study poison-dart frogs. When he told me about a trip he and three other scientists had taken to Suriname, I knew the story would make a terrific book. So over the next few weeks, I interviewed Ron Gagliardo by e-mail and by phone. I also borrowed the journal he kept during the trip. Besides learning more about his trip, I learned a lot about him.

"I also interviewed Robin Saunders, a scientist who worked with Ron Gagliardo. She collected photographs from the trip and now does slide-show presentations. She works at the Newport Aquarium in Newport, Kentucky."

Ron Gagliardo's journal is a collection of facts about the frogs and his own reactions to life in the rain forest.

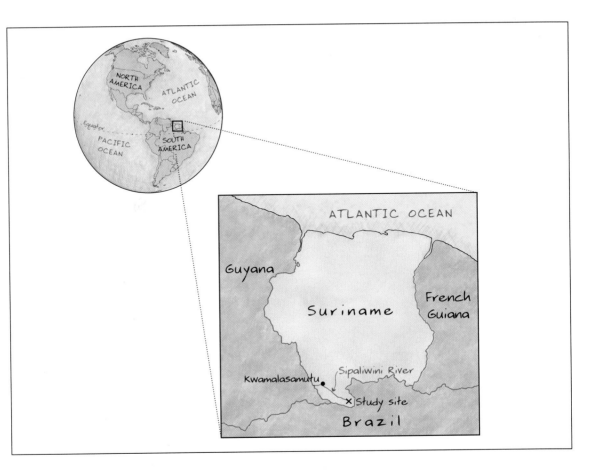

Before Ron Fridell could begin writing, he needed more background information. He spent many hours at his local library reading about the country of Suriname and the poison-dart frogs that live there. He also spent many hours at his computer searching the Internet. "I was amazed at how much information there is on poison-dart frogs on the World Wide Web," he says.

After all this work, Ron had some great material for a book, but he still felt like he needed one more thing. He wanted to see some living poison-dart frogs.

"While searching the Web," Ron recalls, "I visited several sites created by people who breed poison-dart frogs in the United States. One of these sites led me to Greg and Amanda Sihler who breed poison-dart frogs in Tempe, Arizona. I decided to pay Greg and Amanda a visit. They have dozens of these brilliantly colored frogs in terrariums," says Ron. "They truly are amazing to see."

Greg and Amanda Sihler breed frogs in this laboratory in Tempe, Arizona.

Three-quarters of Suriname is covered by mountainous rain forest.

The Adventure Begins

A single-engine plane touches down on a grassy airstrip, and four *wildlife biologists* from the United States step to the ground. The scientists have come to Suriname, a country in northern South America, to search for blue poison-dart frogs.

There are more than 100 kinds of poison-dart frogs on Earth. Most are between 1/2 and 3 inches (1.3 to 7.5 centimeters) long. They live in the lowland forests and rain forests of Central America and South America, where the weather stays warm and *humid* all year long.

Many animals protect themselves by blending in with their surroundings, but not poison-dart frogs. Their bright colors warn other animals to stay away. If a *predator* tries to eat a poison-dart frog, it may die. Even if the enemy lives, it will remember the terrible taste and never eat another poison-dart frog.

Some kinds of poison-dart frogs are in danger of disappearing from Earth forever. The frogs live only

Producing Poisons

- Poison-dart frogs have special skin *glands* that produce poisons. These poisons protect them from their enemies and keep harmful bacteria from multiplying on their skin.

- After living in a zoo or aquarium for a few months, a poison-dart frog loses most of its ability to produce poisons.

- A poison-dart frog born in a zoo or aquarium does not produce any poisons. However, if that frog is released into a rain forest *habitat*, it will soon become poisonous.

- Scientists believe that the insects poison-dart frogs eat in their natural habitat make it possible for the frogs to produce poisons.

- One kind of poison-dart frog can produce enough poison to kill twenty men. In Colombia, South America, a few native tribes still use this poison on their blowgun darts when they hunt.

- The poisons made by some kinds of poison-dart frogs contain chemicals that can be used to relieve pain and prevent heart attacks.

Cutting hardwood trees from Suriname rain forests leaves fewer places for wildlife to live.

in the tropical rain forests of Central America and South America. When people destroy these forests, the frogs have no place to go. They have trouble finding food and a place to lay their eggs.

The wildlife biologists have come to Suriname to help save these *endangered* animals. They will collect some blue poison-dart frogs and bring them back to the United States. The frogs will be kept in a safe place, such as a zoo or aquarium. Scientists will study the frogs to learn more about what they eat and how they behave.

The scientists hope the little blue frogs will like their new home and will *breed*, or produce young frogs. If the wild frogs mate and lay eggs, some of the young tadpoles can be taken to other zoos and aquariums. Then people all over the world will have a chance to see these very special *amphibians*.

What Is an Amphibian?

Poison-dart frogs are amphibians. So are toads, salamanders, and strange wormlike animals called caecilians (si-SIL-yenz). All amphibians hatch from eggs laid in water or on moist ground. Young frogs are called tadpoles. Tadpoles look like fat little fish. They live in water and breathe through gills. As the tadpoles grow, they lose their tail and develop legs. They also lose their gills. Most adult amphibians live on land. They breathe through their skin and lungs. The series of changes that an amphibian goes through to become an adult is called *metamorphosis* (MET-a-mohr-fuh-sis).

The team of wildlife biologists is made up of scientists from two zoos, an aquarium, and a botanical garden in the United States. The scientists have special permission from the Suriname government to collect ten pairs of blue poison-dart frogs. But they still need permission from one more person. They have flown to the village of Kwamalasumutu to meet that person—the chief of the Tirio Indians.

Jack Cover, Anthony Wisnieski, Robin Saunders, and Ron Gagliardo (left to right) have come to Suriname to collect poison-dart frogs.

Meeting the Chief

No animal may be taken from this part of Suriname without the chief's approval. If the chief agrees to let the scientists collect frogs, he will also help them hire guides. These guides will take them deep into the rain forest and help them find the frogs.

The Tirio chief is waiting for the scientists in the village. He knows why they have come. People from a group called Conservation International (CI) have told him about the team. CI is one of several worldwide organizations working to save endangered animals and their habitats. They help scientists do field research in remote areas.

The people working for CI make sure that the local people understand and approve of what the researchers are doing. Three members of CI have come with the scientists to act as *translators*. They will also go into the rain forest with the team.

The meeting gets off to a smooth start. The chief recommends some of his tribe members as guides. In fact, a dozen men from the village have already left in dugout canoes. They will meet the team at a spot up the river.

But when the scientists ask for permission to collect blue poison-dart frogs, the chief is not sure. There is a problem. *Smugglers* have been stealing poison-dart frogs from the rain forest. These smugglers ship the frogs out of Suriname and sell them illegally as pets. Since they take the frogs secretly, no one knows how many blue poison-dart frogs have been smuggled out of Suriname. How many are left? Can the chief allow any more frogs to be taken?

The chief and the scientists agree to keep in contact by two-way radio. When the research team gets to the rain forest, they will find out how many frogs are there. Then they will radio the chief with the news. After he hears from the team, the chief will decide whether the tiny blue frogs can go the United States.

Smugglers have captured many blue poison-dart frogs in Suriname.

The team climbs back into the plane, wondering what they will find in the rain forest. As they fly over the river, the scientists are fascinated by what they see. Miles and miles of flat grassland and mountainous rain forest spread below them. There are no roads or cities in sight. They are a long way from civilization.

As the scientists came in for a landing, they saw this view of the Suriname countryside and the Sipaliwini River.

First Camp

In the early afternoon, Ron, Robin, Jack, and Anthony land on another grassy runway. This airstrip is surrounded by dry, flat grassland. A nearby river winds its way to a distant mountain range. Thick islands of rain forest dot their grassy slopes. Tomorrow the scientists will travel up the river to explore these rain forests. This is where they hope to find poison-dart frogs.

After the scientists unload their equipment from the plane, they take a look at their first campsite. It's an old abandoned building with crumbling, moss-covered wooden steps. They haul their gear inside the building.

They soon discover they are not the only ones seeking shelter here. Tarantulas and cockroaches crawl across the floor, and bats hang from the ceiling. This sight would scare most people, but these scientists are fascinated. They spend their lives working with all kinds of animals. The scientists watch the animals closely, making notes and taking pictures.

The Guides Arrive

Later that day, twelve native guides arrive in four dugout canoes. The scientists speak only English and the guides speak only Surinamese, so the translators from Conservation International help everyone get acquainted.

Most of the Kwamalan guides are wearing rock-band T-shirts, shorts, and blue jeans from the United States and Europe. The curious scientists ask where the guides got their clothes. The translators say they

were given out by Catholic missionaries who set up a school in the village. Only one guide, Amachina, has traditional Tirio Indian clothing. He wears an orange beaded armband on one arm, and a blue beaded armband on the other. A bright red *loincloth* is wrapped around his hips.

When night falls, the four wildlife biologists climb into hammocks they have strung up in the building. They lie awake thinking about what the next 3 weeks will be

Amachina's traditional Indian clothing is ideal for Suriname's hot, moist climate.

The guides, translators, and scientists launch their boats into the Sipaliwini River.

like. They have been on trips like this before and know they are about to have a great adventure.

They also know that it will be tough going. Every day will be hot and humid. They will wear the same clothes every day for 3 weeks and bathe in muddy rivers. They will battle clouds of mosquitoes and may encounter poisonous snakes. They will eat beans and rice for breakfast, lunch, and dinner. They will sleep in hammocks covered with mosquito netting. The scientists will love the adventure, but they will miss the comforts of home.

In the morning, everyone helps load the canoes with equipment and supplies. Then they launch their boats and start down the river.

The lower the water level falls, the harder everyone must push the boat.

Down the River

The team and their guides and translators spend the next 2 days cruising down the Sipaliwini River. They are headed for the western slopes of the Four Brothers Mountains. The journey is not a smooth one, however. It is August, Suriname's dry season, and the water level in the river is very low. For long stretches of the journey, everyone has to wade in the water and push the boats. At night, the group—exhausted from a day of hard work—camps next to the river.

The days may be long, but they are never boring. There is an incredible sight around every bend in the river. Brightly colored macaws fly across the cloudless sky while deadly fer-de-lance snakes slither through the thick grass along the shore. Sometimes the boats are stopped by tall trees that have fallen across the water. The guides move quickly to clear away these obstacles, so the boats can continue floating downstream. Despite these difficulties, everyone seems to enjoy their work and does everything with enthusiasm.

The Struggles of Research

Meanwhile, the scientists are running low on energy. The sun is beating down, and the humidity is rising. They are not used to the clouds of mosquitoes that follow them around or the hard physical labor of traveling down a tropical river. By the time they reach their second campsite, they are tired, hungry, and sore.

The guides set up camp along the river, building shelters from tree branches and palm leaves. Iwan, a CI translator, has caught fish from the river. He smokes them over hot coals to preserve them. Now they can be saved and eaten in the days to come. Aneil, another translator, does the cooking. As always, beans and rice is the main dish. Iwan's smoked fish make a delicious addition.

Without fish caught from the river, there would nothing but rice and beans to eat.

Aneil cooked the same meal every day—for breakfast, lunch, and dinner

When night falls, everyone bathes in the river. Tomorrow the team will hike into the rain forest for the first time. They climb into hammocks strung between trees and draped with mosquito netting. The four biologists do not sleep well. They are used to soft, comfortable beds.

Howler monkeys use their tails to hold on and slow themselves as they leap from branch to branch.

Across the Grassland

The dry slopes of the Four Brothers Mountains are dotted with islands of lush rain forest.

At dawn, the adventurers wake to the roaring cries of howler monkeys. The scientists stumble out of their hammocks. They are still tired, but they can't afford to give in to their weariness. Their real work is just about to begin.

The scientists see the Four Brothers Mountains in the distance. It will be a long, hot hike from the river.

This blue poison-dart frog stands out from its surroundings.

The mountainsides are mostly dry, treeless grassland. Here and there, a stream runs down a slope and an island of green rain forest appears in the yellow grass—like an oasis in a desert. These rain forest islands are mini-jungles. Each one is only about 1 mile (1.6 kilometers) long. This is the only place in the world where the blue poison-dart frog lives.

The blue poison-dart frog ranges in size from 1.5 to 2.5 inches (3.8 to 6.3 cm) long. Its skin has several shades of blue—from a pale powder blue to a dark cobalt. Its poison leaves a terrible taste in the mouth of any predator that tries to eat it, but the poison is not deadly. The blue poison-dart frog eats termites, crickets, ants, and fruit flies. The frog catches these insects with its long, sticky tongue.

A Long Hike

Everyone in the group loads equipment and supplies onto their backs and sets out across the grassland. After a hard, 8-hour hike, they arrive at the foot of

Jack Cover makes notes in the rain forest.

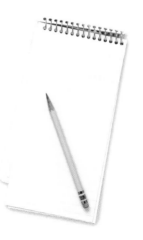

the mountains. One of the scientists has been here before. Jack came here a year ago to study the rain-forest habitats of blue poison-dart frogs. He made careful notes of his observations.

The team wants to see how much the area has changed in the last year. Are the mini-jungles still dense and wet enough to support blue poison-dart frogs?

During the next 3 weeks, Ron, Robin, Jack, and Anthony will examine the areas Jack visited last year. They will also search for new habitats that support blue poison-dart frog populations.

The scientists will pay close attention to what they see and take careful notes. They will use thermometers to keep track of air temperature and barometers to record humidity. They will also photograph the frogs and their habitats.

The team has a *global positioning system (GPS)* device to pinpoint the location of each habitat. The GPS works by bouncing signals off *artificial satellites* that are orbiting Earth. The same kind of device is used by people fishing in unfamiliar waters and by hikers on remote trails.

The research team will use GPS equipment to locate the habitats Jack visited a year ago and mark the location of any new habitats they discover. After a meal of beans and rice, they gather their equipment and set off into the rain forest.

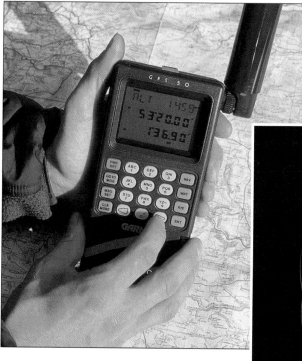

This hand-held GPS receiver (left) uses signals sent by artificial satellites that operate in six different orbits around Earth (below).

Robin Saunders walks into a rain forest island.

Into the Rain Forest

At this point, the biologists split into two search teams. Ron pairs up with Robin, and Jack pairs up with Anthony. Ron and Robin work well together because they have different specialties. As a zookeeper, Robin knows a lot about amphibians. Ron's specialty is tropical plants.

Each team takes along several guides and a translator. That way they can cover more ground. The scientists begin by checking the old sites to see if frogs still live there. The frogs are hard to find, but that doesn't mean their population is low.

The frogs are hiding to protect themselves from the weather. This is the dry season, and the ground is dry and hard. Poison-dart frogs must keep their skins moist, so they stay out of the sun when the ground is dry and the air is hot. On some days, the temperature in the rain forest reaches 120 degrees Fahrenheit (49 degrees Celsius). This means the teams must work extra hard to find the frogs' hiding places.

These field researchers and their guides know the best spots to look. Like detectives hunting for clues, they search beneath rocks, under rotten logs, and around tree roots—anyplace where something tiny might be living. They also peer into the leaves of *bromeliad* plants. The curved sides of bromeliad leaves can hold water like a cup—even after everything around them has dried up. Frog mothers sometimes put their tadpoles in these leafy cups for safekeeping.

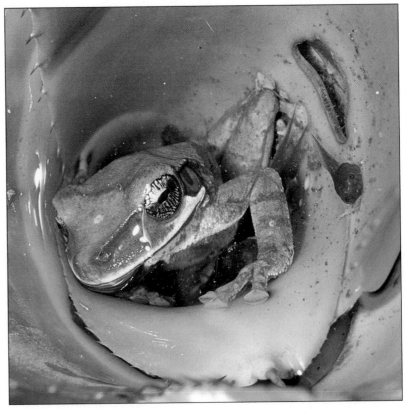

A curled-up bromeliad leaf provides shelter for this frog and her tadpoles.

Picture-Perfect Parents

Poison-dart frogs mate several times a year. The male attracts the female by sitting on a leaf and calling. His calls are a series of peeps, buzzes, and chirps. The female responds to these calls by rubbing up against the male. Then the frogs do a little dance, dipping their heads and arching their necks.

After the dance, the female looks for a moist place to lay her eggs. She lays them under a leaf or a log or in some other well-protected spot. Then the male *fertilizes* the eggs.

Poison-dart frogs take good care of their young. After the eggs hatch, one parent carries the tadpoles on its back. The parent looks for a puddle or some other wet spot where the young will be safe. The female brings the tadpoles food every day.

The tadpoles feed on insect *larvae* and sometimes eat unfertilized eggs. It takes the tadpoles about 3 weeks to change into adults. Then they hop out into the rain forest to start life on their own.

From a Scientist's Journal

All scientists make detailed notes in a journal so that they have a record of what they see. During this Suriname trip, Ron writes in his journal every day. His notes show the ups and downs of field research. On some days the researchers get lucky.

"Entered forest and started working our way up a dry stream with many large boulders," Ron writes.

"We went farther up the stream to the top of the rise. I found a juvenile frog under some palm leaves. Guides found two frogs. Robin found three adults in bromeliads. Returned to camp via boiling hot grassland! Other group found twenty-four adults and two tadpoles."

On other days they aren't so lucky. "We walked through many swamps, including a swamp the size of a football field! No frogs," Ron writes. "Then we walked through dry forest. No water

Ron Gagliardo will use the notes he makes during the journey to learn more about poison-dart frogs.

except in a large stream. No large boulders, not many palms or bromeliads. No frogs."

But lucky or not, every day in the field brings surprises. "Kupias [a guide] saw a jaguar today! And Iwan [a translator] found a really beautiful owl. It was probably a baby because it still had a few down feathers. Took photos."

Iwan's owl looks straight into the camera lens.

Some days are harder than others. "Previous night's rain soaked all my stuff and made sleep impossible. Hard hike back to camp. Some parts of grasslands were so barren I pictured us walking across the moon. I still can't believe we made it back in one piece."

And some days are set aside for rest and relaxation. "Day of rest. Sore throat. Actually slept a good part of the night. Washed clothes, swam. Nice day of recharging for everyone."

But of all the days and nights in the rain forest, one day stands out above the others. On that day, Ron and Robin see a rare and wonderful sight that makes all their work worthwhile.

A Day to Remember

This extraordinary day begins in an ordinary way. Ron and Robin search a dry streambed all morning long without success. They haven't seen a single frog. The temperature is rising. The humidity is high—and getting higher. Robin looks up and sees clouds rolling in. She describes what happens next:

"The sun vanishes," she says, "and the forest becomes silent as the rain moves in. The only sound we hear is huge water droplets colliding with leaves of every size and shape."

Ron Gagliardo:
Wildlife Biologist

Ron Gagliardo grew up near Everglades National Park in southern Florida. When Ron was young, his dad worked for the telephone company. He often brought home frogs and snakes he found while he was repairing telephone lines.

"My dad wanted to get me curious about amphibians and reptiles so I would find out more about them and share my knowledge with him," Ron says.

Ron was in high school when he saw his first poison-dart frogs in a pet store. Their brilliant colors amazed him. "This can't be real!" he thought.

When Ron went to college, he studied amphibians and tropical plants. He was particularly interested in *carnivorous* plants—plants that feed on insects and other small animals. Ron developed a new strain of Venus's-fly-trap that he calls "red dragon" for its brilliant color.

Ron has been on many research trips to South America to study poison-dart frogs. "It's hard work," says Ron, "but it's great to get away from all the little stresses back home and stop worrying and just be happy."

Ron now lives in Baltimore, Maryland. He owns a business that grows tropical plants for museums and aquariums.

Two of the many frogs that came out after a storm in the
Suriname rain forest

Robin and Ron hurry to find shelter. They climb up onto mossy black boulders under trees. From there, they can watch the storm and still keep their camera equipment dry. They sit quietly and watch the storm, never dreaming that something wonderful is about to happen.

"Suddenly, from the crevices between the rocks, small blue frogs begin appearing all around us," Robin says. "To our amazement, we find ourselves surrounded by the frogs we have been searching for days to find! As Ron snaps picture after picture, we marvel at the rare and wonderful event occurring before our eyes."

This single-engine plane, which brought the four scientists to southern Suriname, is designed to take off and land in small, rugged areas.

Heading Back

Three weeks after landing at the airstrip in Kwamalasumutu, the scientists are ready to return to the United States. They are taking ten pairs of blue poison-dart frogs with them. After the rainstorm, the scientists had talked with the Tirio Indian chief by radio. Their incredible story assured him that the frog population on the slopes of the Four Brothers Mountains is thriving. There are plenty of blue poison-dart frogs.

But the scientists also realized how quickly every-thing could change for the blue poison-dart frogs of Suriname. The amphibians would die if their rain-forest habitats were destroyed. They could not survive long in the dry grasslands that surround these mini-jungles. These frogs are stranded on their rain forest islands, and this puts them at risk.

Rain forests all over the world are being destroyed at an alarming rate. People are cutting down trees to sell for lumber and burning them to create farmland. If these forests disappear, the unique creatures that live in them will disappear too.

The Frogs' Future

Just before the scientists fly home, they put their ten male frogs and ten female frogs into plastic containers with air holes. The containers are lined with damp paper towels to keep the frogs moist during the flight.

The frogs will be taken to the National Aquarium in Baltimore, Maryland. They will be kept in small aquariums there and fed crickets and fruit flies. Scientists can study the frogs and create conditions that help them to breed. Some of the young frogs will then be taken to other aquariums and zoos so that people everywhere can see, study, and admire them.

This is one of the frogs that the team captured and brought back to the United States.

Important Words

amphibian (noun) a small animal with moist skin that lives part of its life in water and part on land

artificial satellite (noun) an object that has been launched into space by people

breed (verb) to produce young

bromeliad (noun) a tropical plant with tight clusters of long, sword-shaped leaves and roots that get moisture from the air

carnivorous (adjective) meat-eating

endangered (adjective, adverb) in danger of disappearing from Earth forever

fertilize (*verb*) to bring a female's eggs in contact with a male's sperm and create new life

gland (noun) a body part that releases a fluid

global positioning system (GPS)	(noun) a worldwide navigation system that uses radio signals broadcast by artificial satellites to pinpoint locations
habitat	(noun) a place where a plant or animal lives and grows
humid	(adverb) containing a large amount of moisture
larva	(noun) the first stage in the life of some animals. The plural is *larvae*.
loincloth	(noun) a garment worn around the hips
metamorphosis	(noun) the changes an amphibian goes through as it grows from larva to adult
predator	(noun) an animal that hunts other animals for food
smuggler	(noun) a person who steals something and secretly takes it to a different country
translator	(noun) a person who changes the words of one language to another
wildlife biologist	(noun) a scientist who studies living things in their natural setting

To Find Out More

Books   Cherry, Lynne and Mark J. Plotkin. *The Shaman's Apprentice: A Tale of the Amazon Rain Forest.* New York: Gulliver Books, 1998.

Dewey, Jennifer Owings. *Poison Dart Frogs.* Honesdale, PA: Boyds Mills, 1998.

George, Jean Craighead and Gary Allen. *1 Day in the Tropical Rain Forest.* New York: Ty Crowell, 1990.

Miller, Sara Swan. *Frogs and Toads: The Leggy Leapers.* Danbury, CT: Franklin Watts, 2000.

Stille, Darlene R. *Tropical Rain Forests.* Danbury, CT: Children's Press, 1999.

Organizations and Online Sites

Conservation International
http://www.conservation.org
Site of the nonprofit conservation organization that worked with the wildlife biologists in this book.

National Aquarium in Baltimore
http://www.aqua.org
Site of the aquarium where blue poison-dart frogs from Suriname are being captive-bred.

The Poison-Dart Frog Webring
http://home.wish.net/~waizfisz/frogs/webring.html
A list of links to websites about poison-dart frogs.

Poison Frogs
http://arizona.speedchoice.com/~vwalsh/
A site about captive breeding of poison-dart frogs.

Wildlife Conservation Society
http://www.wcs.org
Site of the nonprofit conservation organization head-quartered at New York City's Bronx Zoo. WCS works to save wildlife and wild lands throughout the world.

Index

Photographs©: Alaska Stock Images: 41; Animals Animals: 10 bottom (Michael Fogden), 26, 42, 43 (Paul Freed); Brian Kenney: cover, 33; Dembinsky Photo Assoc.: 10 top (E. R. Degginger), 10 center (Mark J. Thomas); Jack Demuth: 5; Patricia Walsh: 4; Peter Arnold Inc./Michael J. Doolittle: 32; Photo Researchers, NY: 11 (Wesley Bocxe), 15 (Suzanne L. Collins), 24 (Jan Lindblad), backcover, 21, 44, 46 (Doug Martin), 29 left (David Parker/SPL), 29 right (ESA/CE/Eurocontrol/SPL); Photodisc, Inc.: backcover, 1, border art, 9, 14, 17, 28, 31, 44, 46; Robin Saunders: 8, 18, 19, 20, 25, 38, 40; Ron Gagliardo: 7, 13, 16, 22, 23, 27, 30, 34, 35, 37; Visuals Unlimited/Robert Clay: 12.